MW00982402

GET RESULTS THAT COUNT

GUIDE FOR BUSINESS
RESULTS MEASUREMENT

CONNIE SIU, CMC

◆ FriesenPress

Suite 300 - 990 Fort St
Victoria, BC, Canada, V8V 3K2
www.friesenpress.com

Copyright © 2016 by Connie Siu
First Edition — 2016

All rights reserved.

No part of this publication may be reproduced in any form, or by
any means, electronic or mechanical, including photocopying,
recording, or any information browsing, storage, or retrieval
system, without permission in writing from FriesenPress.

This book is available at special discounts for bulk purchases for
educational, business, fund-raising or sales promotional use. For
more information, please email info@cdcsynectics.com.

Meter graphic by Patrick Trouvé from the Noun Project
Measuring tape graphic by Musket from the Noun Project
Author photograph by Don MacGregor

ISBN
978-1-4602-8121-5 (Hardcover)
978-1-4602-8123-9 (eBook)

1. *Business & Economics, Management Science*
2. *Business & Economics, Training*

Distributed to the trade by The Ingram Book Company

*This book is dedicated to those who seek to raise
the bar for results that really matter.*

TABLE OF CONTENTS

INTRODUCTION

RESULTS REPORTING HAS ALWAYS been an important business management routine. Every month, results are compiled, distributed, and analyzed. Financial results are looked at closely. Unfavorable results are diagnosed for cause and subsequent actions are taken to correct course. Non-financial results are also reviewed to gauge how well the business performs different activities.

Dashboards and reports are used to summarize the results. The abundant volume of data available provide a rich source of information for a company to learn about diverse aspects of its business.

Over the years, I have come across hundreds of reports. Some are simple one-pagers summarizing key results. Others are detailed reports showing a lengthy list of performance indicators. Despite the advance of tools for reporting, challenges with results measurement are common:

- Results are not useful for decision-making
- Measures are too complicated for deriving action
- There is little confidence in the results presented
- Inconsistent definitions are used across business units
- Measures are poorly defined

- There are disconnects between results and strategy
- Measurement does not drive the desired behavior
- There is general fear of criticism

In my past life as a Financial Analyst, I spent twenty-five percent of my time compiling and analyzing results every month. Though the end product was a simple one-page report, I needed to involve others. I relied on the managers for the most up-to-date information in order to reconcile the data extracted from the accounting system and to explain performance variances. Not many of them were thrilled to see me around month-ends. The time commitment is significant. Why should companies invest the effort if the aforementioned challenges continue to lurk around?

"The pause for reflection helps you think through which results are truly pertinent."

My goals with this book are to share my observations and shed some light on how best to utilize results measurement to improve business performance. It will serve as a guide highlighting the essential elements for results measurement.

This book addresses six common questions that managers have about results measurement:

1. What is important and relevant to measure?
2. What are the different types of measures?
3. How to develop meaningful measures?
4. What to do if data are not available?
5. What is the strategy for communication?
6. How to drive accountability?

You will find pragmatic tips and techniques that you can apply. My challenge to you is to pause every now and then to reflect on the results that you monitor every day. Be prepared to question why you need to look at particular results. The pause for reflection helps you think through which results are truly pertinent. In turn, you will end up with relevant results monitoring that leads to higher business performance.

01 PURPOSE OF MEASUREMENT

EXECUTION WITHOUT RESULTS MEASUREMENT is like gambling with time and money. Results are important indicators of how well a business fares. Without results measurement, a business would not be able to tell whether it invests its energy in the right places or makes progress in the right direction. It is detrimental to risk invaluable resources on irrelevant work.

> ### "Execution without results measurement is like gambling with time and money."

Good measures, and hence, measuring the right results, provide insight for modifying strategies and tactics. Poor measures, on the other hand, trigger inappropriate responses.

Proper results measurement provides:

- A gauge for testing assumptions
- A warning for performance deviation
- A supporting fact for decision-making

- A signal on what is not working for a cease and desist decision
- An indication of what is going well to validate the effort spent
- A proof of capabilities to justify further investment
- A representation of performance for comparison with similar businesses
- A focal point for improvement
- An identification of a best practice primed for replicable success
- A starting point for assessing change impact
- A reliable performance baseline for future reference

The above list shows that there are many uses for results measurement. They span from understanding causes of problems to ammunition for action. A business can use informative results to make fact-based decisions. The insight raises confidence in its choice of action. Results measurement is a feedback system. The key purpose of results measurement is to monitor outcomes.

The outcome you want to monitor could be a direct or indirect effect of specific activities. The relationship between cause and effect reveals the pivot points for business management.

"Measuring everything in sight is not beneficial."

The biggest challenge with measurement is determining what to measure. Measuring everything in sight is *not* beneficial. In reality, a business would not have the time and energy to do so. It is the pertinent and rational measurement that offers useful insight for informed decision-making.

As a manager, you are held accountable for the performance of your team. The results you need to focus on might change from time-to-time. Daily efficiency is essential to satisfy customer needs. Capacity utilization is crucial to the capability to handle growth. Cost is a priority during poor economic times. Errors are detrimental to productivity. Incompatibility of the team members is a damper to morale. Each represents an aspect of managing your team and its work.

It is important to know your priorities, what works and what doesn't so that you can best leverage the resources you have. Results monitoring provides the data to support your actions.

02 RELEVANCE

MEASURE FOR MEASUREMENT'S SAKE is unproductive when the data don't provide meaningful information you can act on. This is a key reason why hundreds of report are produced to suit a one-time need. For those who are responsible for slicing and dicing the data, it is frustrating.

To determine what is relevant to measure, you need to be clear on three things:

- Company's strategy and results
- Team's mandate and boundary
- Outcomes and drivers

COMPANY'S STRATEGY AND RESULTS

For many companies, the vision and the mission statement capture the general direction for the business. These broad statements unfortunately are not specific enough for line managers to grasp the implied results.

While senior management pours hours of discussion to develop the strategy for the business, they distil everything into broad, nebulous statements. The insightful details are lost and buried in binders that don't get shared with the rest of the company. The communicated strategy statements are vague messages that most would get the gist of the general meaning, but that might be all.

"As a manager, you need to seek out the *results* **implied in the strategy statements.**"

As a manager, you need to seek out the *results* implied in the strategy statements. Without knowing what the specific results are, it is not possible, and there is perhaps no point, for you to do any planning. Your plan might conflict with the company's strategy.

For example, a company has a strategic goal to be innovative with products and services. What is considered as "innovative?" It could imply three things:

- Develop brand new products and services that don't exist today
- Create a new twist on how the service is delivered
- Enhance the functionality of an existing product

To develop brand new products, research and development are needed. To create an innovative approach to deliver a service, a technology investment might be necessary. The funding needs vary. Undoubtedly, the respective impact on the company's top-line and bottom-line could be night and day.

Without knowing the business intentions, you might be trying different ideas that misdirect the investment of your time and effort. You can only align your actions to support those intentions properly when you know the specific strategic results that are applicable to your team.

TEAM'S MANDATE AND BOUNDARY

The mandate for your team determines what you are accountable for. In order to deliver exceptional performance, you need to understand the correlation between your mandate and the company's strategic results.

Most companies have a functional organizational structure. It seems self-evident that marketing is accountable for the strategies and tactics to reach the target markets, and human resources is accountable for hiring talent and employee training. However, you need to get to more granular details with your mandate.

> *"... to deliver exceptional performance, you need to understand the correlation between your mandate and the company's strategic results."*

If you were the marketing manager, which market segment(s) would be your priority? Within the target market segment, are there customer groups that the company would not want to spend any resources on? How about risks that the company would be willing to take in the pursuit of a new market segment?

The answers to these questions mark the boundary of your playing field. These are issues associated with the mandate that you ought to be aware of. If they are not defined for you, find out from your manager. Otherwise, you might be surprised when the results you acquire are not in line with management expectations.

OUTCOMES AND DRIVERS

Now that you're clear on the company's direction, your team's mandate and the boundary of your 'playing field,' you are ready to identify the results that you must pay attention to.

At the high level, you might be given a revenue or expense target. Your challenge is to deconstruct these high level results to produce outcomes that are meaningful to your work.

The key is to correlate cause and effect. The effect is the end result you aim to deliver. The cause encompasses actions to be undertaken. The causality relationship reveals the roadmap to success. You identify the drivers that influence outcomes. These drivers are the pivots you would manage to elevate performance.

For instance, an operations manager is assigned an expense target for the coming year. The target represents four percent growth. It is great news but the manager needs to see how the budget growth could be translated into higher productivity, a broad business strategic imperative. He needs to consider what drives productivity for the team. The understanding enables that manager to hone in on the right activities.

"... the drivers that influence outcomes are the pivots you would manage to elevate performance."

For results monitoring, you want to examine both the drivers and the outcomes. This is where you need to distinguish the measurement of outcome from action. The next section explains the types of measures and their differences.

03 TYPES OF MEASURES

THERE ARE MANY LABELS for the different types of measures. There are measures for input, output, outcomes, and activities. Some are called lead indicators while others are considered lag indicators. Others are labelled milestones, key performance indicators and indices. It could get confusing.

In general, there are two main groups of measures: action and outcome. Action measurements allow you to monitor the activities you perform to deliver the end outcome. Outcome measurements reflect the end result you achieve. One focuses on the means; the other on the ends.

The table below illustrates a list of sample measures used by different job roles.

Job Role	Measures for Action	Measures for Outcome
Plant manager for a production line	• Overtime pay • Water consumption for cooling	• Backorder • Cost per unit
Insurance adjuster for residential claims	• Average number of site visits per claim • Wait time for repair estimates	• Value of claim settled • Time to settle a claim
Project manager	• Milestone met • Number of issues outstanding	• Project completion • Savings achieved
Team lead for engineering consultants	• Frequency of correcting design errors • Time spent on administration work	• Percentage of hours billable • Client satisfaction
Manager for a call center	• Number of calls abandoned • Percentage of calls for Tier 2 support	• Customer satisfaction • First call resolution rate
General manager for a business unit	• Spend on marketing • Shipping cost	• Revenue • Operating margin

You align the outcome measures with the results you are accountable for and you use action measures to manage the work that needs to be done.

"By scrutinizing the true purpose of work, you identify the outcome that is worthy of the effort."

From the list of sample measures for the various roles shown, you might note that each measure is an indicator of performance:
Measures such as:

- water consumption for cooling, and time spent on administration work are input measures—they capture the materials and effort devoted to do the work
- the value of claims settled are output measures—they capture the quantity of products or value delivered by completing the work
- the wait time for repair estimates are process measures— they reflect the elapsed time for an intermediate task in a process
- the number of issues outstanding are lead indicators— they offer proactive, preventative and predictive insights on potential setbacks on the project completion date
- revenue and operating margin are lag indicators—they provide data on the general result but little information on what contributes to the level of performance
- the number of calls abandoned are resource planning measures—they are statistics useful for planning the number of staff needed for a shift

It doesn't matter what label you want to give the measure. The key point is to distinguish action from outcome. Action is wasted effort if the result is not achieved. By scrutinizing the true purpose of work, you identify the outcome that is worthy of the effort. In turn, you will be able to determine the result you want to measure.

"The segregation of measures into action and outcome measures is a simple way to get clarity on the results you are accountable for."

It is important to note that there is a direct correlation between the action and the outcome each role is responsible for.

Plant managers are accountable for matching production with orders and the cost per unit. To deliver the performance targets set for the production line, they need to ensure each shift is staffed optimally so that there is no need for overtime; and the water consumption is not excessive as the water bill makes up a significant proportion of the production cost. Managers must be cognizant of the effects of inadequate staff levels and the water utilization at different phases of the production cycle. If not, backlogs and high utility costs could result.

For the insurance adjuster, he or she is responsible for minimizing the amount of claim value and closing each claim as quickly as possible. In order to deliver these outcomes, the adjuster would allow legitimate claims only and be persistent in expediting the turnaround time in working with sub-contractors. Otherwise, costs will go up.

For the project manager, the ability to complete a project on time is important. What's more important is to ensure that the anticipated savings for the project are achieved. Despite the latter outcome usually not being known until months later, it is the only way for a business to determine the return on the project. To meet the project completion outcome, the project manager needs to monitor issues resolution and the intermediate milestones. Those two measures signal a need to take prompt action when things are falling behind.

For the engineering consultants team lead, maintaining a high level of billable hours and the quality of work must meet or exceed the client's expectations. To deliver on these two outcomes, the team lead needs to monitor the time spent on administration work as well as project delays due to correcting design errors.

The manager of the call center is accountable for customer satisfaction and resolving their issues on the first call. Hence, he or she needs to monitor how many calls are abandoned, one of the key sources of customer dissatisfaction, and how well equipped his team is in addressing customer inquiries. A high percentage of calls requiring Tier 2 support reflects more training is needed.

The general manager is responsible for the revenue and margin of the business unit. In order to bring in the revenue and maintain a high margin, an adequate budget for marketing will need to be allocated and shipping costs monitored.

The segregation of measures into action and outcome measures is a simple way to get clarity on the results you are accountable for and things you would do and monitor to acquire these results. The thought process lays the foundation for measures development.

04 THE 3 COMPONENTS OF RESULT

MANY OF US ADOPT a brainstorming approach to determine what to measure. We do research on common industry measures, then determine whether they are appropriate for our business. This might get you a list of measures that could be useful, but might not be the best if you want to manage critical activities and drive high performance.

There is a systematic approach to develop performance measures. There is a difference between "selecting" and "developing" measures. Selecting a measure is to scan a list and pick the measures that look relevant. Developing a measure is to identify the result and determine how best to reflect it.

There are three components to a 'result.' They are:

Outcome—the characteristics of the result

Measure—what you use to reflect the outcome

Performance level—a reference point for comparison purposes

It is important to note the distinction between the three components. Mixing them up would cloud the thought process for developing sound measures.

"... mixing up outcome, measure and performance level would cloud the thought process for developing sound measures."

For example, a typical statement about performance is, "We want to achieve 15% cost reduction by the end of the year." The statement has incorporated many things. It describes a performance target. It contains all three components of 'result.' Cost reduction is the outcome. Cost is the measure. The performance level is 15% reduction. A timeline is also included in the statement. This is a fairly straightforward way to describe the desired result and the target performance.

Alternatively, if a company wanted to "attract more talent," it is not as straightforward to determine what to measure. The outcome is to 'attract more talent.' What is a good measure for that? Would the number of job applicants be a good indicator? How about the performance level?

Let's assume you are the manager for the client support center for a software company. We will walk through the steps to identify the results that are relevant and important. This involves defining the three elements of result.

The three steps are:

1. Identify business outcomes

2. Develop measures

3. Define performance level

OUTCOME

Starting with the mandate for your team, determine the business outcomes you need to deliver.

If you were the manager for a client support center, your mandate is to provide excellent support to every client. Identify the characteristics of excellent support. They include:

- Complete response to each inquiry
- Courteous interaction
- Minimal wait time
- High client satisfaction

To identify the outcomes, think about the characteristics of the results. There is a tendency to describe the things you might do to achieve the outcome. For example, you might describe the first outcome above as "provide a complete response to each inquiry." Note the difference in the language used. Clear outcomes are those that reflect what is being delivered.

It's likely that you have more characteristics that you want to include in the list. It's fine to list them all but select the top three or four that are most representative of the excellent support that you want to achieve and hence, monitor.

MEASURE

Assuming the above characteristics are most important, you develop the corresponding performance measures. The respective measures could be:

Business Outcome	Outcome Measure
Complete response to each inquiry	First call resolution
Courteous interaction	Rating on call interaction
Minimum wait time	Call wait time
High client satisfaction	Client satisfaction

In choosing the measures for the business outcomes, keep them simple so that the readers can grasp the meaning. Complex measures such as indices are usually difficult to explain. They also take more effort to compile.

"... actions are the drivers for the outcomes."

For business outcomes that are difficult to quantify, think about what would reflect the characteristics of that outcome. You could use observations or other things that closely associate with the outcome as surrogate measures. Make rational assumptions and test them as you analyze the results.

A distinction you need to make is to segregate the actions from outcomes. As discussed in the section on the types of measures, actions are the drivers for the outcomes. They are the activities that you must focus on and monitor to deliver your mandate. They are on your radar to scrutinize if things are not going smoothly.

After you have developed the outcome measures, you need to identify the drivers that influence how successful you are with the business outcomes. These drivers are areas where you want to invest your energy to ensure everyone on the team is aligned. They are the critical success factors.

"To manage the actions, you also need to monitor the actions for effectiveness."

To identify the drivers, consider the actions that could be undertaken. Determining what actions to take usually is the easy part, the more challenging piece is to ensure that there is a direct correlation with the business outcome. To manage the actions, you also need to monitor the actions for effectiveness.

Let's apply the thought process to each business outcome.

1. **Complete response to each inquiry**

   To provide a complete response to each inquiry, the support rep needs to be knowledgeable about the software so that she can troubleshoot quickly. Failure to do so would result in directing the call to Tier 2 support. Poor first call resolution rate reflects that the support center reps lack expertise. Providing more training might help.

   The driver to develop knowledgeable reps is to provide training. It is not adequate to introduce any kind of training. You need to validate whether the training is effective. In this case, tracking the number of training hours as a measure for the training action is not very useful. Instead, it is more revealing to test the rep after the training. A better approach would be to monitor the test scores. The test score would be the measure for the training action.

2. **Courteous interaction**

   To deliver courteous interaction with clients, the reps would be coached to use the right language and tackle confrontation objectively.

   The action to improve this outcome is to provide coaching but you need to monitor how effective it is. One way to monitor the effectiveness of coaching is to listen in to the calls live or listen to the recording. The measure that reflects the effectiveness of coaching is the number of calls with unfriendly language.

3. **Minimum wait time**

   To minimize the call wait time, you need to staff the support center adequately. Given the random nature of the incoming client queries, your staff level is estimated based on a target level of service. When the level of service is not met, customers will need to wait in queue longer than planned.

   The action to reduce wait time is to staff adequately. What you would monitor is the percentage of calls queued longer than the target queue time. A persistent

pattern of queue time longer than target provides a good
indication that the staffing level needs to be adjusted.

4. **High client satisfaction**

For high client satisfaction, there are many ways to
deliver this outcome. They include addressing each
inquiry fully, doing it quickly, and staffing the support
center adequately to minimize wait time.

These actions are to be monitored. The measure for
'addressing each inquiry fully' is first call resolution. The
client is happy because he or she won't need to call back.
The measure for 'doing it quickly' is average time to solve
an issue. The measure for 'minimum wait time' is call
wait time.

In the following table, the actions that you need to take to
deliver the business outcomes, and the corresponding measures
are summarized.

Business Outcome	Outcome Measure	Action	Action Measure
Complete response to each inquiry	First call resolution	Provide training that sticks	Test score on knowledge after training
Courteous interaction	Rating on call interaction	Provide coaching	Number of calls with unfriendly language
Minimum wait time	Call wait time	Staff adequately	% calls queued
High client satisfaction	Client satisfaction	Provide complete response to each inquiry Solve issue quickly Minimize wait time	First call resolution Average time to solve issue Call wait time

Thought Process

The example illustrates how to develop the measures that align with your mandate and the causal actions that you execute and manage to deliver the outcomes. Take note that the thought process goes from left to right.

It is important to segregate actions from outcomes because it drives clarity on the end goals and the means to get there. Often, we dive right into what we could do and neglect to give sufficient forethought on the outcome that we seek. This leads to taking on actions and initiatives that have little correlation to the target outcome.

The causality relationship between action and outcome also demonstrates the linkage between lead and lag indicators. Outcome measures are lag indicators. Action measures are lead indicators. A lag indicator can be a lead indicator for another outcome. For instance, first call resolution is a lag indicator for test score on knowledge after training. However, it is a lead indicator for client satisfaction.

In managing the performance and activities of your team, you need to have a good handle on essential causality relationships and the important distinction between action and outcome.

PERFORMANCE LEVEL

To set the target performance level, you need to have an idea on what the current level of performance is. For the measures that you have developed, tabulate the results for the past year. They should provide a fairly good snapshot of where you stand today and a baseline for setting performance targets. You could also reference industry benchmarks to gauge what is a reasonable competitive performance level.

"Setting an aggressive target without committing the needed resource is counterproductive."

Using the above example, the target performance level for the each outcome measure could be:

Business Outcome	Outcome Measure	Performance Level
Complete response to each inquiry	First call resolution	95% of calls
Courteous interaction	Rating on call interaction	90% with Very Satisfied rating
Minimum wait time	Call wait time	95% of calls < 25 seconds
High client satisfaction	Client satisfaction	95% Satisfaction

In setting the target performance level, take into consideration what is needed – the time and effort – to deliver the result. Setting an aggressive target without committing the needed resources is counterproductive. You risk setting yourself up for failure. If the target performance level is assigned from top-down, you usually have an opportunity to appeal your case if it is unreasonable. When there is no flexibility, it is good to flag the challenges so that there is an awareness of the risks.

As you define the three components for each result that you are going to monitor, you need to ask constantly why the result is important. This is the best way to challenge your thinking about what is relevant. Trivial measures are easy to identify but they might not take you to where you want to be. Exceptional performance is achieved when you have the right focus. So picking something random to measure does not help to align your actions with the goals you want to achieve.

05 IMPORTANT CONSIDERATIONS

"Each measure and the result you report on encompass a message."

EACH MEASURE AND THE result you report on encompass a message. Your message should be relevant to the audience and something you both care about. This is the litmus test for relevance. In developing your approach to results measurement, it is necessary to incorporate four important considerations. They affect the choice and the detailed composition of the measures and results.

AUDIENCE

The audience for the results includes interested stakeholders outside the company and internal users within the company. External stakeholders could be customers, shareholders, and regulatory bodies. Internal users could be senior management, peers, and staff.

As a manager, you want to ensure that your customers, both external and internal, are well served. At the same time, you want to optimize the performance of your team. The results you want to monitor and the message you want to communicate to the different audience groups may vary.

"If you need to use different measures for external and internal reporting, keep them simple so that it is easy to correlate them."

For a human resources manager, the retention rate is an indicator on how well the company retains its talent. The attrition rate, on the contrary, represents those who choose to leave the company. The ideal situation is to have a high retention rate and low attrition rate.

If you were reporting to the external stakeholders, you likely would use the retention rate, which lends a positive perspective. The attrition rate tends to have a negative connotation.

For management purposes, the attrition rate is more useful. Further, you want to understand the different reasons for departure. Departures could be attributable to retirement, voluntary resignation, or non-performance. In analyzing the reasons for departure, you would be able to identify appropriate actions for improving the retention rate.

In this case, the outcome measure for the human resources manager is the retention rate. He or she would use it for all external and internal reports. In managing the retention rate, other measures might be added to monitor the reasons for departure. These additional measures could be a breakdown of the departures by reason. In reporting to his or her vice president and peers, these additional results would be shared to alert them on situations that require attention.

Let's assume that departure due to non-performance is higher than desired, the manager would need to review the company's hiring procedures and make modifications. This action, if carried out properly, would help to reduce firing due to non-performance. The non-performance departure in turn becomes an action measure.

The audience is a consideration because you want the measure to be meaningful. If indeed you need to use different measures for external and internal reporting, keep them simple so that it is easy to correlate them. Regardless, the measures need to be indicative of the results.

NUMBER OF MEASURES

"If you monitor too many things, some of them will fall off the radar."

Measurement consumes time and effort. You could measure everything but it is not necessary. It is more beneficial to prioritize the results and focus on a select number that have the greatest impact on the outcomes.

There is no rule on how many is an optimum number. However, I will offer the following:

- At the corporate level, determine the most important results that correspond to the strategic goals. If you have more than twenty corporate performance measures, you have too many.
- At the operations level, pick two to three results for each area/department/team that represent its mandated performance. Ensure that these results correlate to the corporate strategic results.

- For each mandated result, identify the critical activities that drive performance. Monitor those critical activities.
- For a project, determine the business outcomes it aims to solve and develop the corresponding measures for the results. Beyond the typical financial benefits, the project might deliver other improvements that you could measure. Don't underestimate those.

From a practical perspective, you want to limit the number of measures so that you are able to manage the activities that drive the result. By using sound measurement, you could pinpoint the root cause of problems and take prompt actions.

If you monitor too many things, some of them will fall off the radar.

PERSPECTIVE

To bring life to a result, you need to pay attention to the composition of the measure. The right perspective brings context to relevance.

"In designing the measure, it is important to consider what would be the most meaningful way to reflect the message you want to communicate."

For each result, there are many ways to present the numbers. You could:

- Use absolute value
- Compute the change in absolute value or percentage
- Present the value as a component of the whole to show relative significance

- Contrast one result with a related result in a ratio
- Compare the same result with another business unit
- Rank a result using a qualitative scale

Each approach calls for different data for the computation. In designing the measure, it is important to consider what would be the most meaningful way to reflect the message you want to communicate.

The human resources manager might choose to show the retention rate as a percentage of the full time equivalents (FTEs). For the breakdown of attrition by departure reason, he or she might look at the actual count for each departure reason and compare the count against other reasons. It might be helpful to look at how significant it is relative to the total new hires.

Perspective can be utilized to emphasize a message, which helps the audience to appreciate the context and make better decisions.

VISUAL PRESENTATION

The popularity of gauges, traffic lights, and graphics has introduced some distraction to the whole reporting exercise. The improper use of visuals actually diminishes the message you want to convey and in some cases, generates confusion. If the readers cannot grasp the message at a glance, it is a pretty good indication that the presentation is not clear.

"... improper use of visuals diminishes the message you want to convey and generates confusion."

TIPS

- Group the results that have a causality relationship together. It helps to provide better context and insight on the overall picture. By placing these results close to each other, it helps the readers keep a coherent thought process in developing the follow-up action.
- Use a table to display non-numeric scores and when there are few columns and rows. Anything bigger than a 5 by 5 will get unwieldy.
- Use a simple line graph to demonstrate trends when the time element plays a role in understanding the direction of progress.
- Use a pie chart to illustrate relative proportions when it is important to convey the significance of specific results. Combine the insignificant proportions to minimize clutter as they carry little weight in your message.
- Use a bar chart for simplicity. It is most effective when used to compare and contrast results.
- Use a scatter plot to show the correlation between two things, or the lack thereof.
- Use colors to highlight and contrast results that you want to draw attention to. Conversely, too many colors become a distraction.
- Select an appropriate scale for the chart to properly reflect the magnitude of variation. The visual message could be skewed otherwise.
- Use a gauge or traffic light to signal a warning. A gauge or traffic light takes up space and adds nothing when the result could be shown in a table or chart.
- Avoid using a three-dimensional bar chart or radar graph. They are difficult to read and make the interpretation challenging.

- Avoid adding decorative elements for they add clutter and little value.

In presenting results, keep it simple. There is no requirement for fancy or complicated graphics. Your goal is to have the readers grasp the message instantly. Including more is not always better. A cluttered report or dashboard screen is a major turnoff to the readers. If more details are needed, provide them on a separate page or the capability to drill down electronically.

By giving due consideration to these four areas, you refine the measures. Tailoring the message to what the audience cares about helps to focus on what is relevant. Limiting the number of measures facilitates prioritization. Getting clarity on the perspective hones the essence of the message. Selecting the proper visual presentation highlights the right emphasis.

06 **THE DATA**

DESPITE THE VOLUMINOUS DATA most businesses have archived, data remain a constant challenge to results measurement. You might find yourself in one of the following situations:

- There are multiple sources for the data
- Data from different sources don't align
- Data are not current
- Data are incomplete
- Data are not accurate
- There is little confidence in the data
- Lack of useful data
- No data available

Data from different sources could produce results that are difficult to reconcile. I have sat through results review meetings where the participants debate intensely about the data source and undoubtedly, the conclusions drawn. This unproductive use of time happens in many companies.

Having good data is important, but the lack of them doesn't mean that your hands are tied. The most important question you need to address is what data would provide representative results. The definition of the measure specifies the data required.

The availability of data could lead to refinement of the chosen measure. There is an interdependency between the two.

There are two ways to deal with the data challenge. They are:

1. Initiate data gathering when there is a lack of data.
2. Create consistency when there are inconsistencies.

DATA GATHERING

When there are no data available, you need to determine how best to gather them.

Manual data gathering might be a start if the effort is not too onerous. Though it sounds tedious, it is straightforward once you set it up. An advantage with starting fresh is that you can make adjustments to the data gathering effort quickly if there is a need to tweak the measure.

Alternatively, explore whether there is a simple way to add the data field(s) to an existing application. This could require engaging the IT team. As there is usually wait time for resource assignment, it would take more time to set up the system to capture what you need.

There is also the option to look for proxy data. This works when the proxy data have a strong correlation to the data you need. You might need to make assumptions or adjustments to the result. Essentially, this will produce a surrogate measure for the result.

"Accuracy is not a necessity when what you need is a homogeneous reflection of performance."

The key for data gathering is to have a solid understanding of the result you intend to measure. For the insurance adjuster example used in Chapter 3, let's assume the company has no systems capability to track the elapse time for settling a residential claim. It has to gather the data manually.

The most direct approach is to have each adjuster track the start and end dates of each claim. The tracking is fairly straightforward. Alternative, the company could extract two dates from the claims system and use them as proxy start and end dates. These proxy dates are not exact but could be adequate for the purpose of that measure.

Consistency is important for data gathering. While accuracy is crucial for measuring results associated with manufacturing and other specific applications, it is not a necessity when what you need is a homogeneous reflection of performance.

CONSISTENCY

The data warehouse has become a vault for archiving data from all the different applications used in a company. It provides a central repository for data. Unfortunately, it doesn't solve the inconsistencies in the data captured through diverse applications. If you have ever attempted to reconcile results produced by different applications, you will appreciate the extensive effort required. Is the effort justified?

It is more beneficial to identify the best source of data and make rational adjustments where necessary.

To determine the best source of data, consider:

1. **Use of the source application**
   By revisiting the purpose of the application, it helps to determine whether the data you seek are core data elements. Core data for an application tend to be complete and consistent.

2. **Completeness**
   This refers to the collection of the particular data fields. If they are gathered for every customer, transaction, month, or other common denomination you need, you have a

dataset that allows you to draw representative insight. Otherwise, it is difficult to make meaningful conclusions.

3. **Timeliness**

   Historical information is good for reflecting on past performance. Data for the past year normally offer a good base for understanding baseline performance. Historical data are excellent for trending analysis. However, what you need going forward is to assess how quickly the data are refreshed in the source application so that you can monitor the result in a timely manner. The measure you choose and the measurement frequency determine the need for timeliness.

4. **Ease of access**

   This impacts the speed of results compilation. It is faster to extract data from one source. In the event that the data are to be extracted from multiple sources, the effort to assemble the data could involve onerous work. The data analytics and reporting tools available today can help ameliorate the challenge.

5. **Accuracy**

   The degree of accuracy needed varies with the nature of the result and its use. Accuracy is impacted by how the data are captured. Identify anomalies in the data and determine their impacts. Depending on the purpose of the measurement and how you use the results, less than perfectly accurate data could provide a reasonable indication of the result and trend.

Once the data source is selected, determine if it is necessary to make assumptions and adjustments to allow for the imperfect data. Do a reasonableness check of the results.

"The key is in the consistency of your input data and the interpretation of the results."

Working with imperfect data is not an issue when you can make allowances for it. By applying a consistent approach to the computation and the analysis, you establish a reliable reference point. The key is in the consistency of your input data and the interpretation of the results.

To get buy-in from others who use the results, share the information on the data source and justify the need for adjustments or assumptions. When you have alignment, imperfect data becomes a non-issue.

07 COMMUNICATION STRATEGY

COMMUNICATION OF THE RESULTS is just as important as how you select measures and compile results.

The effects on the receiver of the information differ with the content, context, and how it is delivered. After all, you want to share the results because they are important.

To create the desired effect, you need to pay attention to three aspects:

- Message
- Frequency
- Medium

MESSAGE

The content of the message must be relevant to the receiver. In general, present what is needed to convey the message you want to share. Providing too much detail can lead to information overload. Sharing too little does not explain the context.

External stakeholders such as investors would like to understand whether the results are trending in the right direction. Internal customers want to see that the agreed upon service levels are met. Your team wants to know whether it is successful in meeting expectations. Your manager is keen to know about overall performance and trending. You will want to understand the level of performance and the cause for any deviation from the target level.

"For internal communication, you want to share as much as possible as it will encourage others to pay attention and collaborate."

As you are accountable for the performance of your team, you need to have a good handle on the contributing factors to success, as well as the stumbling blocks that have a negative impact on the results. Be prepared to provide a solid explanation for the results. The best practice is to be open about the positives as well as the negatives. After all, you are doing a disservice to the company if problems are swept under the rug. You could be more reserved about the communication to the external audience groups. For internal communication, you want to share as much as possible as it will encourage others to pay attention and collaborate.

FREQUENCY

With respect to the frequency of communication, you determine what is appropriate for the receiver. Quarterly communications to the external stakeholders might be sufficient for information purposes. For internal stakeholders, monthly communications are typical. You might communicate quarterly if you want to avoid knee-jerk reactions. Note that measurement frequency doesn't need to be the same as the communication frequency.

For active monitoring of critical activities, the communication should be as regular and frequent as you need to take prompt action. This is a key reason why the linkage between action and result needs to be clearly understood.

MEDIUM

There are many ways to communicate the results. Your goal is accomplished when the receiver of the information understands the message and takes the desired action.

For your team, it is most effective to communicate the results face-to-face. This allows you to draw attention to specific results. It also provides an opportunity to have a dialogue on issues that need to be addressed and the follow-up action. The personal approach sends a message that you care.

> ## *"Your goal is accomplished when the receiver of the information understands the message and takes the desired action."*

In sharing results with peers and other departments, a mix of media could be used to suit the needs of each area. Electronic communication saves time but there is a high probability that the receiver misses or ignores it. For results that you want others to take action, you need to to ensure that the message is heard and understood.

Effective results communication is more than broadcasting. The effort of results measurement is futile when there is little interest in taking action about the outcomes.

08 ACCOUNTABILITY FOR ACTION

SOUND MEASUREMENTS ALERT YOU to take action. They serve as an early warning system.

Upon setting the target performance, you need to have a plan that includes:

- Actions that are effective
- Individuals or team best suited for the work
- Support effort needed
- Finance and time commitment

This action plan encompasses the roadmap to deliver the results. Undoubtedly, the effort should be commensurate with the gap between the baseline, your performance today, and the target.

DELEGATION

As you delegate the work to your team, it is of the utmost importance that there is an explicit dialogue on expectations and the ownership of the results. Keep an open mind about any concerns raised. It is your responsibility to ensure that there is acceptance of the assigned target. .

"... it is of the utmost importance that there is an explicit dialogue on expectations and the ownership of the results."

When the result comes in better than the target for the period, determine if it is worthwhile to take advantage of the momentum. On the contrary, identify the issues that you need to tackle if the result is not up to par. The crucial effort in taking the time to follow up with your team allows you to stay the course. Failing to follow through to ensure that issues are resolved leads to delays and certainly would not improve the situation.

For work that requires cross-departmental collaboration, it is helpful to have a mutual understanding with your counterpart(s) on the importance of mutual contributions. The key is to obtain the alignment ahead so that if a problem arises, you get the cooperation you need.

SUPPORT

While your team diligently carries out the work, you monitor the results. It is within your management realm to provide any assistance along the way. The support could be in the form of budget allocation, shift of manpower, or a sounding board. Employing a 'sink or swim' approach does not work because your team's failure is your failure.

Be mindful of shifting targets. The shift could be triggered by a change in market dynamics or business requirements imposed by regulatory bodies. This is a landmine for confusion. It is likely that when you receive a directive to change course, you need to juggle your team to accommodate the shift. It is important to ponder how the shift impacts your ability to meet the target performance. It is a matter of priority and it is reasonable to challenge why the shift is necessary. Your team will sure question you, so you better be prepared to address that.

> ### *"Employing a 'sink or swim' approach does not work because your team's failure is your failure."*

It is unfair to hold someone accountable when indeed, they are not equipped or are unable to focus their effort. It is your responsibility to delegate the work to the appropriate people and provide any support needed to make it a success.

09 A FEW CHALLENGES

RESULTS MEASUREMENT IS MORE than a reporting exercise; you aim to measure the right results for the purpose of driving focus on the activities that count. There are several challenges that might set you off on a tangent.

BENCHMARK RESULTS

It is a common practice to compare a company's performance with another in the industry. Is there any chance that you are comparing apples and oranges? There are many factors that affect the comparability of results.

1. **Business strategy**

   The target market, products and services offered by each business are unique. Though they might have generic similarities, the differences in the market segment, and the variation in the product mix affect the results. Hence, the benchmark result could be, at best, used as a reference only. For instance, it is not meaningful to compare the ratio of labor to total revenue for a niche software engineering company with the average ratio for the entire software engineering industry. There is such a big range for the labor rate and software prices.

2. **Operations**

Technology has afforded businesses to operate effectively using innovative operating models. Companies can hire the talent to do the work in-house, outsource the work, or use supplementary resources on a contractual basis. Each of these options has a different cost structure. Companies with extensive mechanized systems would be more efficient than the lesser ones. It is difficult to look at the benchmark figures alone and do a fair comparison.

3. **Results compilation**

The formulae used to compute the benchmark result might not be clearly defined. In order to generate comparable figures for your business, you need to understand the specifics incorporated in the formulae, the assumptions, and the data. This requires extensive effort. Without the proper research, you would not be able to adjust your data and normalize the results. The comparison would not be meaningful at all.

Benchmark results do not provide the best yardstick for comparison especially for measures that are generic and draw on a broad selection of businesses. Measurement at a more granular level is usually more useful. For example, revenue per square foot, a popular benchmark measure in the retail industry, is crude. Cosmetic revenue per square foot is better as you narrow the product range and the business focus. Even then, any difference in the brands carried will skew the results.

If your performance is pegged to any benchmark result, you need to do the due diligence and understand the compilation of the benchmark result. The understanding will enable you to formulate an appropriate explanation for any gap.

FINANCIAL RESULTS

Every aspect of running a business has a direct or indirect link to the company's top-line and the bottom-line. Financial results are relatively easy to obtain from the accounting system. But financial results are lag indicators. By the time you review the numbers, it is usually too late to do anything about them.

"By the time you review the financial results, it is usually too late to do anything about them."

For managers who are accountable for bringing in revenue, revenue is the ultimate outcome measure. At the same time, they need to identify the activities that are the key drivers for achieving the revenue target. The tendency is to list way too many things they could do and lose sight of what is most effective. The trick to avoid missing the forest for the trees is to define sound action measures. The thought process discussed earlier will help to filter noise.

For managers in the support functions such as finance and supply chain, their teams serve other areas in the business. How effectively they do their job constitutes success for the company. Hence, the primary measures for them relate to how they do their work. Financial results are secondary.

For example, the supply chain is responsible for the acquisition of materials and labor necessary to produce and deliver the products and services to the customers. Its work has a direct link to cost. However, carrying out the sourcing activities as efficiently as possible is also important to avoid delays and opportunity costs. For the supply chain manager, focusing on financial measures alone is inadequate.

Similarly, the finance department is responsible for accounting, billing, payroll, and more. It is an essential part of a business. The department represents an administrative cost on the income statement. Its cost is important but the financial result for this department is not the primary focus. As the mandate is to be accurate and timely with its work, the key measures would be around these two important aspects.

Avoid using the financial results as the default. Instead, seek relevant results that pertain to the purpose of the work.

LINE-OF-SIGHT

As action-oriented individuals, employees act with good intentions to do what they believe is best for the company. The action might not be fruitful when it contravenes the strategic direction for the business.

"Without the line-of-sight to the big picture, it is easy to slip into an internally focused mode."

Does your team have clarity on how its work relates to the company's success in the big scheme of things? Did you take the time to explain the linkage? Did your vice-president provide clear guidance on where to focus your time and energy? Without the line-of-sight, it is a hit or miss game.

For instance, there is a directive to reduce the departmental expense by 15%. To be fair, you figure that it is best to apply the same reduction across all the teams you manage. You anticipate that this approach would be unlikely to trigger any complaint. Let's assume you are the manager for customer support. There are two channels, namely the contact center and web support. It would not be wise to reduce the headcount for web support when the company is in the midst of expanding its online services.

Many decisions, big and small, are made by your team members in doing their job every day. You need to educate them continuously on the company's evolving strategy. Without the line-of-sight to the big picture, it is easy to slip into an internally focused mode. The narrow view shifts priorities, leading to conflicts. You certainly don't want to waste energy on misconstrued priorities.

CULTURE

Many shy away from results measurement because of the negative perception around blame. Subsequently, there is a tendency to report what is positive and a strong desire to minimize the exposure of poor results. The fear of looking bad leads to the undesirable behavior of sweeping problems under the rug. This becomes a ticking time bomb.

"Work processes cross departmental boundaries. Collaboration is needed, not competition."

There is also a belief that measurement is fair only when it is within one's control. This leads to the silo mentality. When employees are focused on work within their work boundary, they might seek to optimize results at the expense of another work group. This causes conflicts. Work processes cross departmental boundaries. Collaboration is needed, not competition.

Changing an ingrained negative perception is not easy. It takes time. To foster a positive culture for results measurement, it has to start from the top. Executives and managers must work together to educate the employees on its importance. They need to communicate clearly the purpose of measurement and why it is critical to shine a light on poor results. You need to reinforce the same message regularly and encourage your team to share observations.

A positive measurement culture requires each employee to understand and acknowledge the importance of results measurement. When employees are receptive to performance monitoring, they readily take ownership of the outcome of their work.

10 ABOUT RELEVANCE AND IMPORTANCE

EFFECTIVE RESULTS MEASUREMENT PROVIDES insight on how well your team performs and is an essential tool to hone in on areas that deserve attention. So it is crucial that you measure what is relevant and important.

Start with the mandate of your team and identify the business outcome that you are accountable for. That business outcome should align with the company's strategic goals. In identifying the business outcome, consider why your customers need you. This leads to the characteristics associated with the result your customers expect, which in turn could be the outcome measures.

To deliver exceptional results, there is a need to understand the drivers that impact the business outcome. These drivers have an effect on the speed, quality and the cost of doing the work. They are the action drivers you monitor to attain the target performance. The more clarity you have on the causality relationship between action and outcome, the easier it becomes to isolate what to monitor on your radar.

There are many things you could measure, but the goal is not to measure everything. Do an objective review of the results you are monitoring. Are they still important? If you could not come up with a relevant message associated with the result, it is likely that the result is not important anymore.

When you communicate the results, be selective with how much you want to convey to the audience. The amount of information and the corresponding level of detail to be presented ought to be coherent. The results that you report to the external audience could be at a high level while the results you monitor for day-to-day operations are more granular.

"... monitoring irrelevant and unimportant results is an exercise that brings zero benefit."

A reliable data source offers confidence in the results that you report. However, perfection is not a necessity because assumptions and adjustments could be made to do consistent analyses. The key is to have a consistent view of the results, forming a sound basis for reaching rational conclusions.

The purpose of measurement is to take note of both the good and poor results. By following up with appropriate actions, you will turn successes into best practices and ratify work that hampers performance. The individual who has the accountability for the result has the full responsibility to monitor and make the necessary changes for improvement. The buy-in from your team on measurement is crucial to your success.

In summary, the choice of results measurement determines the focus of your action. That is why it is so important to have a clear understanding of your team's mandate and the line-of-sight to the overall business goals. It is better to have a few quality measures than many random measures that bear little correlation to your mandate. Good measures serve as a voice of reckoning. They shed light on areas that deserve attention. On the flip side, monitoring irrelevant and unimportant results is an exercise that brings zero benefit.

Results measurement calls for an objective assessment of what is important and where to invest resources for optimal benefits.

ABOUT THE AUTHOR

CONNIE SIU IS DRIVEN by her passion for business excellence. For over 25 years she has helped companies build high performance businesses through strategic clarity and operational excellence. Through her management consulting firm, CDC Synectics Inc., she works with business leaders to optimize resource deployment, develop effective best practices, and improve efficiency and profitability.

Connie has authored over 100 articles and continues to share her insight through speaking, her podcast, *Make It Count*, and blog. She is the author of a primer on process, *Enhance Performance through Process Improvement*, and a compendium of articles on operations, *Doing More with Less through Operational Excellence*.

Connie holds MBA, Master and Bachelor Engineering degrees from the University of British Columbia. She is a Certified Management Consultant. Her company is based in Richmond, British Columbia, Canada.

CONTACT CONNIE

CONNIE SPEAKS FREQUENTLY ON the topic of results measurement. She can deliver a keynote, half-day, or full-day version of this content, depending on your needs. If you are interested in finding out more, please visit her Speaking page at:

cdcsynectics.com/speaking

You can also connect with Connie here:

Website: www.cdcsynectics.com
LinkedIn: ca.linkedin.com/in/ConnieSiuWT
Twitter: twitter.com/ConnieSiuCMC

Printed in Canada